Let My Past Be My Past

A True Story

Maria Antonette Finney

Let My Past Be My Past

Moving Forward by Healing from the Past

AND IT WAS BY GOD'S GRACE AND MERCY THAT I'M
STILL HERE!!!!

Maria Antonette Finney aka
Ms. Poochie & Ms. Priceless

Library of Congress Control Number: 2011904517

ISBN-13: 978-1497302518

ISBN-10: 149730251X

This book was printed in the United States of America.

Dedication

First and foremost, I want to thank God. You are my everything. I refuse to let rocks cry out for me. To my mom: You have taught me about life, how to be a God-fearing woman, and a good mother to my children. I thank you for that. God couldn't have given me a better mother than you (I love you Mommy Duke). RIP Daddy. You were a wonderful example of fatherhood and manhood. I remember the good times we shared and no one will ever replace you and you also showed me how a young man is supposed to treat his lady and that's like a queen that I am, and I know if you were still here you would be so proud of your baby girl (I love you Poppa Doppa). Victoria: You are my shining star and my beautiful princess. You gave me hope and the courage to do what I needed to do in life. I had you at an early age, but we grew up together. Lil' Clifford, my handsome prince: I love you, too. You also gave me the courage to write this book. To my middle son, Bernard: You didn't live long enough, but God does not make mistakes. I know that you are in heaven with my Lord and Savior, Jesus Christ. Tavonta, my youngest son: You are so special. At first, I did not think that you would make it, but prayer is powerful! You, too, are my handsome prince. I have one princess and three princes. I love you all. Thank you for your love and support.

Last but not least, to my brother, James. Rest in Peace. I thought we would grow old together, but you got sick and were called back home to be with God. You did, however, leave me with many good memories. I will always love you. And I would like to thank those others MS

VICKEY WORTHY MY SPIRITUAL MOTHER for your support in all areas of my life and for just being there when things start going down as I begin to write on my book and you were there to pick me up. And you were there through it all to give me the support that I need that you were getting from GOD. And for believing me when other's didn't and for calling me out when I was going through and when I didn't won't to tell no one. And to MRS.KEISHA BROWN I want to also say thank you for the numbers of nights that I spent at your house working on my book and the times when you came to my house and helped me write my book as well and for you just being who you are. And for your hubby for putting up with me and the babies too and I will forever but grateful for you all too may GOD bless those that were there with me during my trying times and I love all of you!! I have other brothers, but that is another story. I still love you guys. Look at your little star sister now . . . It's all because of the God in me!!!AND I WILL NEVER EVER FORGET GOD CAUSE IT'S ALL BECAUSE OF HIS GRACE AND MERCY THAT I AM STILL HERE TODAY AND I DON'T WANT TO TAKE NO CREDIT CAUSE IF IT HADNT BEEN FOR GOD WHO WAS ON MY SIDE I DON'T KNOW WHERE I WOULD BE TODAY!!!!!AND THIS ROAD HAS NOT ALWAYS BEEN EASY FOR ME BUT I JUST LIFTED MY HEAD TOWARDS THE HILLS WHERE MY HELP COMES FROM AND I WOULD SAY A SMALL PRAYER TO MY FATHER IN HEAVEN THANK YOU LORD AND I WILL CONTINUE TO BLESS YOUR NAME!!!!

My Prayer of Deliverance for My readers

I pray that this book will help someone who is going through something. I pray that it will give them the courage to keep going and let them know that God will never give up on them. My motto is: "If God is for me, then who can be against me?" Don't ever give up on God because He won't give up on you. He's able to give you the desires of your heart if you will just trust Him. We deprive ourselves of so many things because we are either too proud or too stubborn to ask. Things won't happen when you want them to, but He will come through in the nick of time. Our time is not His time.

I am a born-again Christian who is living life to the fullest by doing the right thing. God has truly saved me from myself. I am in this world, but I refuse to be of it. I strive to be a light in the world and a help to others. I am here to talk about God and how wonderful it feels to be saved and preach the Gospel to the world. Writing this book has allowed me to see how I used to be and how far I have come. For that I thank God all the more. I may not be where I want to be, but I am definitely not where I used to be. For that I thank God all the more.

I pray that this book will be an inspiration to all who read it. As I close, I want to leave something with you about me: "As for me and my house, we will serve the Lord (Joshua 24:15)." "If you make the Most High your dwelling place, then no harm will befall you. No disaster will come near your tent (Psalm 91: 9, 10)."

This book is a true account of the events that have shaped my life. The names of the people involved have been changed to protect their privacy.

AND THAT WHAT GOD HAS FOR YOU IS FOR YOU,AND

DON'T EVER ALLOW ANYONE TO DETERMINE YOUR FUTURE,NOR LET ANYONE PASS JUDGMENT ON YOU CAUSE ONLY GOD SIT THAT HIGH.CAUSE YOU CAN DO ALL THINGS! THROUGH CHRIST WHO STRENGTHS YOU CAUSE THERE IS HOPE,AND ALWAYS REMEMBER THERE IS NO ROOM FOR FAILURE AND THE WORD CAN'T IS NOT IN YOUR MOUTH BE BLESSED AND I PRAY NOTHING BUT GREATEST TO THOSE ALL OVER THE WORLD!!

Introduction

Hello my name is Maria Finney and I was born September 12, 1973 at the Medical Center of Central Georgia at 7:45 AM. I was raised in Macon, Georgia. Although I now reside just outside of Atlanta, Macon is my first love. It has such a rich and fascinating history. It lies on the site of the former home of the Creek Indians. Because of its location, it is nicknamed the heart of Georgia. It is the home of several institutions of higher learning, museums and tourist attractions. The Tubman African American Museum is the largest African American museum in Georgia. I had the pleasure of visiting it several times in my youth. It also has a rich musical heritage. It is currently home to the Georgia Music Hall of Fame. Another wonderful thing about Macon is the annual International Cherry Blossom Festival.

First of all, I want to thank God for His twins, Grace and Mercy. If it had not been for the Lord on my side, I don't know where I would be today. God has been so good to me, and I am a true vessel of Him. That's real talk from my heart. God is the head of my life and I cannot thank Him enough for loving me unconditionally now and forever. God has really shown up and out in my life. I thank Him for that. I have had to go through some hard times, but those trials have made me the woman that I am today. People have said that I would not make it, but look at me now. I am a God-fearing woman and I'm going straight to the top with God's help. (WHEN I LOOK BACK OVER MY LIFE MY GOD MY GOD! HE IS A GREAT GOD AND A GOD OF ORDER. NOW I'M NOT GONNA SAY IT HAS ALWAYS BEEN EASY BUT I HAVE TRAVELED DOWN SOME ROADS IN MY

LIFE. THANK YOU LORD GOD!!!!!!)

In The Beginning

GENESIS CHAPTER ONE

The journey began when my mother (Mary Smith) and my father (James Finney) met through a mutual friend in 1970. They were married in 1972 and I was born in September 1973. My mother was a teacher and my father was a janitor, money was tight back then so my father opened his first boot leg house on Edgewood Ave in Macon, GA; now for those of y'all who don't know what I'm talking about this is a house where liquor and beer is sold illegally, it was also our family home.

My siblings and I attended the *Community Center* after school to do our homework and play. It was our escape from seeing my dad's customers coming and going. I loved going there, we went on different field trips and outings during the summer. It was a place to keep kids off the streets and out of trouble. I remember my first swimming lesson, they put me on the high diving board and pushed me off, and I thought I was drowning. They told me to open my eyes and I noticed that I was on the other side of the pool. Everyone was laughing at me, and at first, I didn't see anything funny. Then I thought about it and began laughing, too! After that, I went swimming every day. I was about six years old, jumping off the high diving board.

A typical day for me usually included school and later, the Community Center. On Wednesdays, I would attend Bible Study. On Sundays, I attended Sunday school and Morning

Service. When we got home, my mother would cook dinner. While she was cooking, we would go outside and play. When dinner was over, my family and I would spend quality time together, and that made me feel so good just to be at home with my daddy and the rest of the family. All we would do is watch TV back then. I remember how I felt bad sometimes after our family time together was over and when it was time to go to bed, I would start crying and my little dog would jump in the bed with me and I would just go to sleep.

Besides attending the Community Center, one of my favorite hobbies was singing. I sang in the choir and it brought me so much joy. I have always been told that my voice was my gift from God, at the time I had no idea what that meant. I can remember that my brother and I use to go to Super Soul Night at the skating rink and our mom use to say y'all been at church listening to the Lord's Word and now you want to go and listen to the devil's music. Y'all should have just stayed home from church." We would look at each other and be like man why she acting like that? But we wanted to still go anyway and at the time, we wasn't listening to that and we went to super soul night.

It was so much fun that we went each and every Sunday. My brothers and his friends would even go to the mall on Saturdays just to buy outfits for Sunday evening at the skating rink. You know they had to be dressed to impress the ladies. They would double and triple date and have a blast. Those were some of the best times of my life. I can remember one time we had gone to the skating rink and a big fight broke out. A young guy was killed and I was like Oh My God, did this really just happen!

Within minutes our mom was there to pick us up and I was much shaken up when she got there. Another time I can recall when we went skating and my brother's skates were yellow and black. They were expensive and he loved them to death. We went skating and once again a fight broke out but this time it wasn't so bad and everyone was told to go outside. He put his skates down because he was flirting or messing with someone and when our mom got there, I don't know what he was thinking but he forgot them. He didn't think about them until we were about a mile down the road and when we turned around and went back they were gone. Our mom was so mad at him. He didn't get no more skates and I felt bad for him because he loved them skates like it was his brother lol! So that was the end of going to the skating rink for us and on Sundays, there wasn't anything else to do but just to enjoy each other and watch movies till it was time to take a bathe and go to bed.

I can remember I was about five or six years old and my parents had enrolled me into a Christian private school. The school was made up of mainly white kids and not many black kids (so y'all already know I was very uneasy about this). On Monday, I wasn't happy about going to school, I was kicking, fighting and screaming cause I did not want to go I was uneasy about starting school because to me home was my comfort zone and I felt as though they were taking me from what made me happy which was playing with other kids and being able to eat as much as I wanted. It made me sad to think about how I would have to get up real early in the morning, get dressed and go out into the cold morning air. So the only way I could become easy with it was when I had seen the other kids, and they were walking up to me and saying hello to me. The next day was another school day and I said my prayers and didn't want to get out the bed, just at the thought of going to school again scared me and I really didn't want to go for sure this time. I was told to get up and handle my business and in ten minutes, it was time to go. We were driving down the street and the school was surrounded by big pretty houses and the people were all white so the neighborhood was really nice and there also was a big beautiful church up the road. I was still having those feelings that I didn't want to go to school. I would miss playing with my cabbage patch dolls and looking at cartoons. We went inside and this tall lady with this wicked grin on her face said good morning, I was like there is nothing good about this morning or any other morning. Yeah I had a mind like a big girl that was who I was back then keeping it real with you, and just looking at her made me so afraid of her that I ran between my mommy legs and held on for dear life. Looking up at her, it was like when she talked I heard something popping in her mouth, I started shaking real bad then and saying with my eyes please mommy don't let this lady get me. As she kept talking, the popping got even louder and she said let's take Maria to her new classroom. I was still on my mommy's legs so she had to drag me down the hall. As soon as they walked me to my class and I sat down for a little while, my mom walked out of the room and I got right up and walked right behind her. So when she got halfway down the hall I knew that was my chance to make a run for it out the door.

I told them that I had to go to the restroom and she pointed me to the restroom, and as soon as I saw a way out the door I was gone and I was able to see the tail end of my parents' tail light and I went to follow the car, I was walking on the sidewalks and running in the streets, cars were honking their horns but I didn't let that stop me, I was gone. I became so tired that I had to slow it down for a few minutes. Then the worst thing happened, my mommy got on the highway and I said to myself what in the world is she doing going on the highway. So back to what I'm saying (I was running on the highway and people then was trying to pull over and get me I wasn't hearing that.) Running on the highway? Clarify that statement. I was still running and crying at the same time and it was kind of cold too and me with my crazy self-trying to catch my mommy on the highway. Then I lost her and I had to get off the highway and plus I was real tired of running behind her and running from the people too.)

I came up on these people who were seated on a bench and some were standing up. I was on Mercer University, now that was the straight ghetto you were bound to see everything on that side of town. People were waiting on something so I sat down with my legs crossed and was sniffing at the same time. I didn't know any of those people so all of a sudden I saw this big bus coming upland. They were crowded around and I got on the bus without the driver seeing me. I went and sat by this old lady and no one even noticed that I was on there by myself so I was quiet and didn't say a word to no one. So we drove by the hood, pass some projects and you could see drug dealers and pimps pushing hoes down when we passed them. We were riding downtown and I remembered my daddy worked down there. I asked someone to pull the string down for me. I got off the bus and walked into the Macon Police Department .The room was big and everybody was busy running around. As I looked around, this white fat bald man came up behind me and touched me on my shoulder. I jumped and said oh my god who are you? I asked where my parents were and that I wanted them now and I started to cry uncontrollable. He took me in his office and I was screaming to the top of my head. I started kicking and my nose was running real bad. The other officer came into his office and they asked me for my info I was giving it to them as fast as they were asking. They weren't able to get hold of my mother so they called my father. They got a hold of him, and they were so happy about me being the age I was to know all my info.

As I waited on my daddy, the officers were so nice to me. They gave me a bag of chips and a Pepsi soda. I sat down with my legs hanging from the seat and I was so afraid that my daddy was going to beat me right at the police department... One hour went by and all of a sudden I heard a man's voice asking where was his daughter and he sounded like he was crying. Then y'all already know I was starting to cry too. He picked me up and was thanking god that nothing happened to his baby girl. The officer came up to him and said Mr. Finney, you have a smart and brave daughter to do and go through what she has been through today. You all should be very proud of her and at the same time I know you all are upset with her too so don't beat her too bad because she thought very fast today. Take her home and just love on her. When we got in the car, I was still crying because I just knew he was going to tear my behind up. He buckled me in and took me home. As time went on, a he stopped and got us something to eat and I indeed thought he was going to beat me, because I had run away from school so I wasn't going to say a word at all.

Well the lesson I learned from that day was that I could have been killed, snatched up or even run over by a car, so now that I'm grown that was very crazy of me to leave a place that my parents knew was good for me. The advice to all the parents: always make sure that you watch your kids and make sure they are in the right place at the right time because life is too short. I can remember when I was very young and I was sick, and my daddy had to take me to work with him (he had one of them kind of jobs that you were your own boss). He was a cab service driver. That was another hustle he had ... my dad was a jack of all trades. He let me ride in the front seat when he went to work so that I wouldn't have to be around or sit next to those folks. My daddy was over protective of me. His boss didn't know that I was with him. He had stopped by the package store after he reported in (now y'all know it's called a liquor store) and he was drinking and was very tipsy. One thing about my daddy is that he could drive well when he was drunk. So he worked that whole day and he didn't care who saw me in the car. He had his baby with him. He put me in the back seat (now I know what y'all thinking now— what was he thinking) so when he went to take the car back . . . yeah my daddy forgot I was in the back seat. Remember he had been drinking all day. He returned the car in at the end of his shift and went home. He got in his car as usual and clocked out and went on home to shower, shave and sit down at the dinner table with his family he thought.

As soon as he got home and walked through the door, my mom and brother was already at home and she was cooking dinner for the family. She asked where was I and he replied ain't she with you? She was with you Finney that's the name she called him when she is pissed with him. My daddy looked like he had just seen a ghost and he was shaking like a bush and he started to look pale. He told her I must be in that damn cab so my daddy called down there and asked was his car still down there. The man said yes that the man who was supposed to drive that night called in sick (now the Lord was working it out in his favor that night) so he asked what was wrong and he only told him he forgot something in the car. Y'all already know my mom was 58 hot with him so when they got back down there, they were running to the car, and my daddy opened up the door and saw I was still sleeping like a princess snoring and all. My mom grabbed me and said "motherfucker I can't believe you left our daughter in the back of the fucking car", with all the yelling I woke up screaming to the top of my lungs and my mom said let's go I can't believe this shit Finney. (((There she go again with that name Finney because she was pissed, my brother said she could have spit fire on him. I was about eight years old and we were still living on Edgewood Avenue and my daddy had a bootleg house (ok we all have had someone in our family who sold liquor in the back of the house during the day and on the weekend) my dad wasn't home I don't know where he was at on this certain day, the police came to our house and I was scared like hell. My mom had just had an operation and could not get out the bed; the officer came in and went straight to my parent's room. He said Mrs. Finney we know you just had an operation and she could not get out the bed. so you can just tell us where the moon shine is (that's that hard strong liquor that will make you blind if you consume too much, and knock you off your feet) now by this time there was police everywhere and people were coming out their houses been nosy as hell. And I was in the front yard looking crazy and not really understanding what was going on, and the TV folks were there and I was on TV and all of a sudden I saw the folks coming off around our house with jugs of moon shine. they not only found five jugs it was like 50 jugs and everybody was like damn I didn't know they had that much Shit my daddy kept the moon shine under the house in the basement and I use to always wonder why they kept going around there. And I was like I bet if they had all that was under our house they would have broken in and stole it all but everyone that came were good friends of the family and they came on a regular to get drink, even when the liquor store was closed and a lot when they were open.

On Sundays they were having a party. Back then, I was too young to ask any questions. That day my mom and I were the only ones there … us and the law. We were on the news that night and they were talking about what they had found under our house. I was standing in the front yard waving at the camera and the police and everyone thought that was funny. (I had the kid's happy meal smile on my face) so later that night my dad came home and my mom was to hurt and mad to curse him out so she said Finney, what the hell is going on again? My daddy had this poise look on his face when she questioned him and I was like wooo my daddy is in trouble again with mommy and the law. But everything got back to normal after a while and daddy was back in business. This time he hide it in a much different place because people might be looking in the same place as last time. I attended B.S. Ingram School on Telfair Street. The neighborhood was okay. There was a lot going on like drunks, whores and drug pushers and you might be coming down the street and see a man hitting on a woman; for me that was the norm so I imitated what I was seeing on my way to school. Every day there was a boy I was beating up (now ain't that backwards y'all). I also threw his book bag in the sewer. I must admit that I had a tendency to be mean. On top of that, I was also a tomboy. I guess my brothers made me that way. My brother and his friends used to beat me up and I would have to fight them back. He used to tell me that if I got into a fight and I lost and came home crying they or he would fight me and send me back out to fight again and again until I won. One day, as luck would have it, I decided to pick on that same kid because he had a speech impediment. He got me good that day!

He threw a rock at me and hit me in my head. My brother noticed it as he was getting off the bus. I thought I was just hot and sweaty, but no, that was blood trickling down my face. It had gotten all over my shirt. I ran home and told my parents who took me straight to the hospital. As I was sitting in the emergency room, I was mad as hell and I said I'm going to get that lil bastard when I get back to school the next day. My parents were so upset, I was crying and my head hurt like hell like I had been hit by a truck. Y'all already know it was time for me to get him and make him hurt like I was hurting. As always it was like my mom could read my mind and she started talking about how God don't like ugly but hell I wasn't hearing that shit at that moment, my head was hurting like hell but when I got home and thought about what my mom had said, that bastard was saved by the bell or should I say by me being afraid to go to hell. The next day, I was planning on getting him back for the rock incident, but I learned my lesson. I learned that I should not pick on people just because they are different and right now, that same lil boy, we are the best of friends today. And now when we see each other, we hug and shake hands like nothing happen when we were kids. Today he is a changed man and he is helping people. His passion is too really help the kids who are in trouble and have been in jail and are trying to get their life in order again. So people if you are ever faced with something like this, never pick at them because you never know their issues and their stories as to why they are like they are. It's not their fault. Never judge a book by its cover.

Some days, I didn't want to go to school. On those days, I would hide in the backyard. When Dad got home, Ms. Evans would tell on me. Now Ms. Evans was the nosey neighbor who told every damn thing. I could have hit her in her damn eye she made me so sick just to see her coming. (When I didn't go to school one day, I didn't see her in her damn window looking at me, if I had seen that nosey witch I would have ran-- These sentence is out of place.) I was trying to skip school one day so I ran behind our home on Edgewood and called myself trying to hide behind it when I looked up and guess who I saw... the nosey neighbor.

She was standing there smiling with no teeth in her mouth. So my daddy came around and got me and here is how the conversation went "Poochie, why you not in school and what were you thinking and didn't you think you would get caught? And do you know who caught you?" I was like our nosey neighbor with this poise look on my face and if looks could kill, I would have killed her right then and there! And the worst thing happened of course, my dad took me to school and I was mad as hell and he told me "Lil girl you better take that frown off your face right now before I have to take it off and it isn't going to feel good by far. So I got my act together in 2.5 seconds and I was ready to go to school. I was still mad at the neighbor, and when I got to school, my belly started hurting like crazy like I had butterflies in it. The people in the front office was happy to see me but I didn't feel the same about them. I don't know why I didn't want to go to school that day. So the school day went on as usual and then it was time to go home. The day went by really fast too.

Even though I was a tomboy, I loved to dress up. I would put on a dress at the drop of a dime but when my mom and I would go shopping on Saturdays, I would still pick out some pants and jeans. Growing up, I had a lot of dogs, so I would dress them up, too. I would walk those dogs down the street like we were performing in a fashion show. I would get up on a Saturday morning and I would tell my dogs (yeah I talked to my dogs like they were human), ok I got our outfits ready to put on, we about to get ready in a few minutes. Then we all would be walking down Edgewood in a straight line and I was the head leader. Although, I had many dogs in my lifetime, one dog in particular was my favorite. Keisha was the best dog I ever had. I treated her like she was a person. I think she thought she was too! She slept with me at night. Everywhere I went, she followed. She was smart, too. One night, my neighbor's house caught fire and she let us know so that everyone got out safely. She was also a good watchdog. She lived with us for many years. Then, one day she got under my bed and died. That was one of the saddest days for me. I still get emotional sometimes when I think of her. (Excuse me for a second I need to get my thoughts together, again she was my heart). After she died, it took a long time for me to get another dog. It took me years before I would accept another dog again, and when that did happen, I cried. I wanted Keisha and not them. When that dog tried to play with me, I would push him off of me. I didn't feel like been bothered, but after some time, that dog would lay in the bed with me after I went to sleep (they knew better) and I would try to roll over but couldn't. I would have this little warm thing up against me and all I could do was grab it, hug it and cry. So I had no choice but to love the dog that they got for me.

My mother was a strong God-fearing woman, who did not take any mess from her children. She nurtured us and taught us how to stay in a child's place. She and I sang in the choir on Sundays. We also sang with other choirs around town. Even as a small child, I understood that singing was a ministry. I also liked to perform in plays and give speeches in church.

One Easter speech in particular stands out in my mind. I couldn't have been no more than six or seven years old. After I had given my speech, the pastor asked me where God was. I replied, "He in the house!" The congregation thought that was the cutest thing they had ever heard. It took them a while to stop laughing. I guess I have always had a knack for making people laugh, even if it was at my expense at times. I look back over my life and just laugh to myself y about how me and my brother use to fight just about every Sunday, and we were fighting about crazy stuff Lord have mercy people.

I can remember when the same brother use to do my hair cause my mom didn't know how to (she use to jack me up) and my daddy didn't either and my brother had to do my hair . He use to put small braids in my hair that was standing all over the place but in the right place. And you talking about that being the funniest thing oh yes he had to do my hair and it was shooting pops all over the place. He thought that was the prettiest thing too. On my way to school looking a hot mess but sometimes I wasn't happy going to school but I had no other choice either, go to school or wear a butt-whipping.

Growing up, I had five good friends with whom I spent much of my time. Their names were Ruby, Mary, Pam, Sue and Ruddy. Now she was the loud one out the group but she was a sweet kid. Her mom had died when she was very young. She was outspoken and we use to fight but the next day we were friends again. Now that's how good friends do (probably because I would always win). We use to go out of town together and she would tell me secrets and I would do the same and we made a pack to never tell no one. She was smart and I would copy off her paper in school and I guess she figured I was cheating off her paper one day and that clown wrote the wrong answer down. Now I didn't know that she had two test papers, one was hers and the other was to mess me up. When we got our papers back, I got an F and she got an A (there went the friendship . . . nah I'm just kidding). Mary, on the other hand, I don't know too much to say about her, only that she always tried to act bad, and she too was a fighter and I use to go down to her house and eat up her food. She use too get mad with me and we would have a food fight. Pam (oh my god she was a hot mess she had lots of boyfriends) so she was a whole lot faster than the rest of us was. Her parents were hard on her. They didn't play the radio and they couldn't stand me, hell I didn't like them either, because they use to tell her that I was a bad because my dad had a bootleg house. Hell while they was tripping on my tip, her dad didn't know that I knew on the weekends he was coming up to our house getting drunk as hell but other than that she was a good friend as well.

Last but not the least Sue; now she was so slow and people use to pick on her and she would get mad and she would cry. Her parents were not together. Her mom had to work crazy end and odds jobs just to take care her and her brother. Plus she was a hell raiser too and she had these crazy boyfriends who would beat her (it was her mom that I saw get beat up). When her mom told them that she was going to call the police, they ran like a crack head. Growing up when you saw one you saw the other (y'all already know that u saw all of us) we were like that fighting packs. We went to school and church together, we spent time at each other's houses on the weekends. The best thing about it was that we enjoyed each other, no matter what it was. We even enjoyed doing absolutely nothing as long as we were together, those were good times that I will never forget.

For as long as I can remember, I have always been a Daddy's girl. Whatever I wanted, I got it. All I had to do was ask, and it was mine. Because I loved him so much, I tried to spend as much time with him as I could. Daddy always told us not to go behind the apartment building because it was dangerous back there because of the high hill. One day, my brothers decided to disobey him just for the heck of it. They got red mud all over them, and I ran inside to tell my mother. When Dad came home, my mom told him what happened, and my brothers got in trouble. My brothers were so angry with me because I told on them. They threatened to retaliate, so I tried to stay close to my dad. Somehow, they caught me off guard and tripped me. I hit the floor and once again, they got a whipping. That night, they planned to get me again, but it didn't happen. We had dinner, showered, and went to bed. The next day, we went to church. Later that day, my older brothers went home to their mother. They didn't live with us.

Even though we had our differences, my brothers were very protective of me. I remember a time when one of my brother's friends and I were playing. His friend pushed me on my big wheel, but he pushed me too fast down the street and to make matters worse, he pushed me down a hill on Edgewood Avenue over Third Street and as a result, I hurt my knee. When my brother got home and heard about it, he tried to really hurt that boy. Eventually, some of his friends came and broke up the fight.

That event made me realize that my brothers would go to the end of the world to protect me.

They use to make me so mad when they saw me they would say Poochie (that was the nickname my daddy gave me when I was in my mommy's belly) your mom, dad or your brother know you down here. I would say nope and they used to send me home crying. I would be like you ain't my daddy, and they used to act like they were coming after me and I would be running so fast like I was a crack head.

One of my favorite people in the entire world was my great-grandmother. She used to come up from Peach County to visit her friend, who was also my neighbor, Ms. Evans the nosy old lady from Edgewood Ave. She was born in the early 1900s and old-school. I loved her so much because we were a lot alike. Our birthdays were only one week apart in September. She liked to dip snuff and I often wondered what that felt like. To satisfy my curiosity, she would sometimes allow me to dip snuff when I would visit her, but I never did it up here I only did it when I was down in Peach County. When my brothers found out, they told my mother, and I got into big trouble when I got home. I can laugh about it now, but it was not at all funny when it happened!

I also enjoyed visiting her on weekends and when school was out for the summer. I would often take two of my best friends and we would have the best time together. I also had a cousin who lived near her, and she would come to visit, too. We would go near the train tracks just to watch the trains pass by. When you are young, even seemingly minor things tend to amuse you and we use to talk to the trains too. I can sit back and laugh about it now. One weekend, I decided to visit my grandmother alone. I just wanted to have some one-on-one time with her. That quality time meant so much to me. But on that particular weekend, tragedy struck. After spending time talking and laughing, we decided that we would take an afternoon nap; now that's one thing she didn't play, you going to lay the hell down and take a nap (and that's what I did to my kids, they already knew two pm naptime). After some time had passed, I woke up first and decided to go outside for a while. I was looking at the people, kids and dogs walk down the streets and Lord have mercy they would stop and talk for hours if you let them. Suddenly, I heard a loud thump and ran inside to see what had happened. My heart was beating real fast. My grandmother had gotten up and she was weak when she got up and she had missed a step and fallen on the floor. When I heard it, I ran in there and she was laying on the floor with no movements. I said to myself Oh My God! Is my granny dead? I was trying to see if I could feel or hear her breathe so I immediately called for help and then placed a call to my mother who was back in Macon. I was right there by her side the whole time just crying.

I remember crying uncontrollably. How could this be happening after such a wonderful day together? She was more than my grandmother. She was like a best friend to me. I was afraid that she would die that day. Thankfully, because I acted so quickly, my grandmother survived that accident. She had lost a lot of blood and would not have pulled through if she had been alone when it happened. So when they (the police and the hospital people) got there and people saw where they were going, everyone ran to my granny's house to see what was going on. They started working on her and they had everything on the floor, and I was like are y'all going to pick this stuff up (cause I knew granny didn't play about her house being dirty). Yeah I was thinking about that too while all this was going on funny huh? And as they were loading her up I was getting her bags with her important info in it and I was getting ready to lock up behind us as well. So while they were working on her in the back I was talking to my mom on the phone, and I told her that I was going to ride either in the front or the back, because I wanted to be right there next to my granny. I was still crying that day because I thought she was going to die on me. So we all left and got to the Peach County Hospital and she had her eyes open just a little bit, and they (the doctors) told me that I couldn't go any farther so I went and sat down and waited on the rest of the family to come down. I was still crying and once again I was mad with God and started asking him why HE was allowing something like this happen, she didn't have a mean streak in her body and she went to church and was in different ministries so I was really confused. So after about one hour everyone showed up and I ran into my mommy's arms just crying so hard and my heart was beating like crazy at the same time. And they went to the front desk to ask about my granny and how was she doing. But they said at the time they didn't have no news, because she was still in the operating room so we all sat down. Four hours had passed and we were all in the waiting room, and the neighbors and friends came to the hospital as well to make sure she was alright.

Finally the doctor came out, we all got up and walked over to him and he was like at first we didn't think she was going to make it, because she had lost a lot of blood. I started crying again. The doctor said she is a strong lady and when he asked who was there with her, I peeked my head through the crowd and said me and he reached out for me. He said that was a brave thing you did young lady and if it hadn't been for you thinking so fast she could have died so he said to my parents I know y'all are very proud of her.

We asked when we could see her and they said in about one hour because she was in the recovery room then they had to put her in her own private room. The adults started crying and I was like she going to be fine but they were thanking God for bringing her through this bad time and for me being there with her. An hour passed and only two people could go in at a time to see her so my mom and one other adult went in. Y'all know I was made like hell I should have gone in first. My mom stayed in there for about thirty minutes then she came out crying, and I was like what's wrong with her? I was like I'm going in next cause that's my granny and everyone was like ok sweetie (I said to myself I know). I went in and what I saw I was like Oh My God! My granny had tubes everywhere and I ran to her bed side. I was crying all over again and talking to her even though I knew she couldn't hear me. I said a short prayer and it went like this: please Lord don't let my granny die. She is the biggest part of the family and is the one keeping the family together. Lord, please don't let her die.

Let her be healed and able to come home to her family. I kissed her on the mouth and said I love you my granny and I will be back in a few minutes. There are more people who want to see you, hold on now you hear me. So everybody waited to see my granny and we were all tired so we went out to eat, went back to her house, took a shower and went to bed. I said a small prayer, watched some TV then I went to sleep in my granny's bed. I slept pretty good and the next thing I knew it was morning again, we took showers, ate breakfast and then we were on our way back to the hospital to see my granny. When we got up there, she was woke and just looking at the TV and she was so happy to see everyone. I ran and got in the bed with her and we just loved and kissed on each other said a soft thank you to God. She stayed in the hospital for a few more days and please believe me, I was right there with her.

When she was released from the hospital, she came to live with us in Macon. I absolutely loved that! It was like having a sleepover with my best friend every night. After a while, though, she had to be moved to a nursing home. My mother was still working as a teacher, and could not dedicate the time needed for her care. The nursing home was right across the street from my mother's school, so it was easy for her to check on her daily. They took good care of her there, which made the transition much easier to handle. I was there every day just spending time with my granny and I didn't want to miss a beat with her neither.

The following summer, my grandmother had to have an operation and I was once again scared and I went to God again and I told Him how I was so thankful for her to be alive and I didn't want her to die but if it was in His will that she go home to be with Him then I respect that Amen. The day before she had to go in the hospital my mommy, my brother and I went to the nursing home and we had a ball, not knowing that day was going to be her last (excuse me again). We went home and did our normal and then we got ready for summer school the next morning. While we were waiting for her to come out of surgery, we received the worst news: Granny had a heart attack and died right there on the operating table. My heart dropped straight down to my feet. You already how I was feeling once again. I was mad at God for taking away my granny. It was like I could not breathe. I just sat there in disbelief. She was gone and there was nothing I could do to bring her back. And though I was surrounded by my family, I felt so alone. I think that moment was the most alone I had felt in my entire life.

We had her body taken back to Peach County for the funeral and burial. That day was so gloomy. The skies opened with thunder, lightning, and rain. It was as if the heavens were crying out just as I was. Heaven had finally gotten its angel back. The pastor gave a wonderful eulogy and the church was filled with the people who knew and loved her the most. After the burial, we all gathered together and celebrated her life. We shared stories, laughter and tears. It was time to begin the healing process and comfort one another. She was an inspiration to me and many others. I will never forget our times together and how I use to go down there and she would come to Macon to visit us.

I did not travel much as a child, but I do remember going to New York with my mother when I was twelve years old. We went to visit my aunt and her family. New York is much different from Macon, Georgia. It was like stepping into a new and exciting world. We stayed for two weeks and we had so much fun. My cousin took me swimming almost every day and I can remember times I use to swim with my eyes open like a fish.

Even though I was used to swimming with my eyes open, I could not do it there because there was too much chlorine in the water and it messed my eyes up real bad. I thought I was going blind because my eyes hurt so badly.

We went back to my aunt's house and got ready for a block party. We had gone out and bought a fly outfit to wear. We were all sitting on the porch and I was waiting on my other cousin and I was hearing all the good music. I first fell in love with hip hop in the early 80's and have been in love ever since then until the day I die. I don't know what kind of music they playing now, it don't have no meaning. I was able to meet singers, rappers and other famous people. I always wanted to be a singer, so you could just imagine my excitement when I actually saw them face to face. When we weren't sightseeing, we enjoyed watching television and sharing stories. I enjoyed myself so much that I really did not want to leave. I was thankful for the opportunity for my mother and me to travel together. So this was our summer break and I wanted to stay longer but I had to get ready for school and indeed I was to be able to tell my friends what I had done over the summertime. I also met this lady and she was a pretty black woman with long hair and she lived by herself and she had these big cats. When I tell you they were big as hell, they looked like rats. She used to sleep with them and they used to be in the bath tub with her. I thought that was the nastiest thing I have ever heard of in my life.

She was a sweet little lady, I dared not to eat anything out of her house. I wouldn't even go inside her house for goodness sake. As we were walking down the streets, we would see rats running away from her house and they were so big but the first time I saw one I went running back towards my aunt's house yelling. They came out the house and said what's wrong? Maria and I said we saw some big rats down by her house running across the streets. We went to the block party that night and that was my first time seeing weave in people's hair, and I told my cousin, her hair was pretty and that's when she said that was a weave in her hair (now y'all already know I was like what the hell) but I said it was pretty anyway and I wanted my hair done before we left to come back to Macon. I got my hair braided and I knew I was the thing . . . I got me a New York hairdo. So the next week it was time for us to leave and I had to say goodbye to all the friends that I had met.

When we returned, the house was a mess! (My brother) had gotten so drunk that he fell and messed up his leg. (One brother or more than one)It wasn't right for me to laugh at him, but I did. That's what he got for getting drunk in the first place! My mom was steaming hot about the whole situation. She made (them) both clean up the house. (My dad and brother) had a party while we were away in New York. Some things were broken and the house was a wreck (I tell u it was a hot mess) my daddy wasn't home when we got there so when he (who is he?)Got there, he was in for a cursing of his life.

I felt so sorry for my brother and I helped him clean up his side of the house (and I was laughing at the same time too) and our dad and my brother kept saying how sorry [they] were (you previously mentioned your dad was not home) and our mommy told him (my brother) that the next time he was going to a friend or family member's house next time.

My friends were so happy to see me when I returned to school. Since I had the gift of gab, I couldn't wait to give them all the details. I told them everything that happened from start to finish. None of them had ever been to New York, so suddenly, I was an instant celebrity! It felt so good to say that I had done something that my friends only dreamed about. I could have talked about my trip all the day long and they had a lot of questions to ask me like . . . did I see any famous people and I was like yeah and I also told them how we went across the bridge over into Brooklyn and we were on the city bus, I actual saw a woman get jacked for her rings and earrings and when she didn't give it up, they tore the earrings off her ear. So I was like darn they are really rough up here and I moved even closer to my cousin and please believe me, we didn't get off the bus in that area.

At the age of 12 years old, I was raped by a friend of the family and he used to be around my older brother who lived in the same house as I did. I was walking home from the community center one night and it had gotten dark. I can't remember where my brother was this night, as I was walking it was dark, cold and the wind was blowing really badly and I was trying to make it in. All of a sudden I hear something out the bushes and it put its big hands over my mouth and it came from the back so at first I didn't see a face only heard a horrible voice. He threw me on the ground and pulled my pants down and raped me over and over again. I don't even know how long because it felt like forever and all I can remember is crying softly and biting down on my lips. And asking God why was this happening to me because I didn't deserve something as bad as this. I was really mad at God. And before he finished, I saw his face and I realize who he was and he threatened me by saying I better not tell a soul not even my best friend. I jumped up and ran in the house, passed my family and went straight in the bathroom to take off them nasty clothes. I turned the water on very hot added a little cold. I was crying still because my private was hurting and this monster had hurt me and he stole something special from me as well. And I knelt down in the corner of the shower and was washing myself off very hard and still crying. I got out of the shower to see that I was still bleeding so I got a pad and put it in my panties and slowly walked in my bedroom. My brother came in and said ma wants to know what's wrong with you Poochie and did you want to eat dinner and I said no. My heart was crying on the inside cause I wanted so bad to tell him that one of the guy's that be around the house just raped me, but I kept hearing his voices saying "you better not say a word to no one" so he left out the room and I cut my TV and lights off and cried myself to sleep. The next morning I didn't want to get out of bed and I was hoping all that had been a bad dream, but when I got up reality set in and my body was hurting very bad and I slowly got ready for school. As I was walking to the bus stop with my friend, I saw him at the bus stop with his kid sister and in my mind I was saying you have a monster as a brother who do bad things to good people. He still had that same look on his face as it was in my dream you better not say a word to no one. And that day, I wanted to walk to school so that's what my friend and I did. I was hurting so bad and he had this smile on his face, it looks could kill he was raping me again. I never told a soul about this and my father went to his grave without knowing and my brother went to his grave not knowing as well. It took years for me to heal and at the end of my book I will give some tips on i f something like this ever happens to you, or a love one or friend . . .

My Pre-Teen years

When I was about 13 years old, I had a friend named Stacey. I would sleep over at her house almost every weekend. Eventually, she met a boy named Bobby and they got along very well. Bobby had a cousin named Billy. We were introduced to one another and we had an instant connection. We became very good friends and later decided to date. We got along so well, that he and his cousin came to see us almost every weekend.

Billy and I did everything together. He and his cousin attended church outings with me but no one ever knew that we had something going on. His cousin, Bobby would come along to the church outings as well even though my friend Stacey went. When he came to see me, I had him meet me at my friend's house because of my father and brother. They were very over protective of me, y'all know what I'm talking about if y'all the youngest kid. I didn't want them to scare him off. We dated for four years before we had sex and I got knocked up the first go round when he took me to my prom I was about five or six months then and everyone came to take pictures of us and the vehicle we were riding in. We all took pictures and my daddy took photos of the car, us and the car tag. My father was very clear that I needed to be back home by midnight. If I wasn't, the police would be called. After the dance, we went out to dinner and some of my class mates we met up at Shoney's and ate dinner, now take in mind I never ate in front of him so I was so very nervous that I ordered too much food. When he stepped away from the table to go to the restroom, I ate like crazy. And when he came back, I was eating so fast and he was like what is wrong with you baby and I whisper in his ears you know I'm eating for two silly and we starting laughing. Everyone was like what's so funny you two love birds and I was like if only they knew. I wasted a lot of money that night cause I hadn't never ate in front of him (that's crazy huh) and as soon as we were done eating we all went to Colman Hills, that's where the lovers go to make out or just go to spend some quality time together, and of course we made out and so did everyone else(oops did I just say that). What the heck we were expecting our first child!!

Billy was very athletic. He played basketball for Northeast High School he had so much potential but he just couldn't seem to stay out of trouble. It didn't matter to me, though. I was head over heels in love with him. And he loved me, too. He would ride his bike from the East Side to Bloomfield just to see me. Now that's what I call true love. I found myself sneaking around with him. I even got bold enough to have him in my house when no one was home.

One night, when I thought we were alone, we got caught red handed. We heard a car door close and I tried to sneak him out the front door. My brother always came in through the side door, so I thought that we would be in the clear. Boy was I wrong. The front door was locked, so when he tried to get out, he ran into the glass door, making a loud noise. He then ran into the television and my brother caught him. I was so scared that my brother would really hurt him. Then my brother went into my parents' room to wake my dad to let him know what I had done. I didn't even know that he was home! My father came out of his bedroom 350° hot. He had steam coming out his head like a red head devil. You could have fried an egg on his forehead. He was actually that angry. He was like a raging bull that night. But I didn't care, we were still together even after all that (I bet y'all saying she bold).

My brother didn't know it at the time, but I was already pregnant with my first child. We drove down to Tampa to help him move into his apartment at his college. I slept for a good portion of the trip. My brother thought that I was just tired but we would stop at the rest areas to move around and to get food and water or drinks. Remember, my parents did not know I was expecting. And I wasn't going to the doctor, I just ate well and rest well. I was so glad that my brother would be going to school in Florida. That meant that he couldn't keep tabs on me.

One of my cravings during my first pregnancy was lemons with salt on them. I would buy a bag of them and just eat them until I got sick. I even had Billy buying lemons and we sometimes would walk to the store together. I would eat lemons, throw up and back at it again crazy huh? I just wanted my lemons and salt. One day, I had gotten sick one too many times and my mother decided to take me to the emergency room. After they ran some tests, they told her that I was expecting a baby. She was so disappointed in me. I guess she wanted more for me. She wanted me to get a good education and experience life before becoming a mother for the first time. When we got home. She called and told my daddy. Shit I was scared. I wanted to pack me a small bag and run away then. My daddy said we are taken her to have an abortion and my mom said what the hell you say? If something happen to her and the baby, that blood will be on my hands. Now this was around the time, the family business started (y'all already know) my dad was so mad with me and Billy. He said he could just kill him for what he did. My mom and I went shopping at the Macon Mall, now that was the place to be, stores and more. You could crazy in there. Now I was almost done at the private school and at that time my dad dope business was up, and he bought me a dog. He was so small but he had big feet so I named him was Bigfoot. Bigfoot and I used to walk down the street and I can remember once we were walking and these two big dogs came from nowhere. Now remember I said Bigfoot was little. He stood in front of me, pushed me down and got over me to protect me from the two big dogs.

He started barking real loud. Our neighbor heard and saw what he did and went to get my family. Now at first they were mad at him and the guy told them what they just had seen. They said Bigfoot is a good watch dog protecting one of his owners. My brother still didn't know I was having a baby and I cut grass and everything I had to have some kind of cover up at first.

On the night I went into labor, my brother and I had gotten into a huge fight over the telephone. We were fussing about something so dumb. He pissed me off real bad and we hung up the phone on each other. Because I did not take any prenatal classes, I did not know what signs to look for when it was time to have a baby. When my pain became almost unbearable, I decided to call my sister-in-law. She told me when I see mucus and blood that I was in labor and that I needed to get to a hospital. I was hurting so bad and I got on the floor, crawled into my parents' room and told them what was happening. My father was so nervous that he could not even put his clothes on the right way. Now that was a funny sight to see back then. My mom called 911. I was so scared and I was hurting so bad, I really had nothing to say then the ambulance came in 20 minutes or so.

When I got into the ambulance, I was terrified. The man said you don't want to lie down and I said no sir that I could not even lie down on the bed. The paramedics asked me if this was my first baby. I explained that it was. I was in so much pain. I thought that she would arrive before we could get to the hospital because she was really trying to push through and I was closing my legs even tighter.

For a while, it was just me and my mom because my dad had to go to work. He told my mom to call him if something happens, or if Poochie have the baby before he gets to the hospital. My mom was there just watching me as I was in so much pain it felt like she was going to tear me apart. Then the doctor eventually gave me an epidural for the pain and I was able to sleep for a while.

About four hours later, the doctor came in to check me and he said she was not ready yet. Honey when they gave me that stuff to clean me out as it was getting closer, I was trying to make it to the bathroom, well I didn't, I messed all over myself and everything else. As I was falling asleep, I felt a whole lot better and then I was gone.

My mom came back in and said how is my baby sleeping through all that pain? And the nurse said about 30 minutes after you left the pain got so great, she was crying so hard and asked if there was anything she could have for the pain so we gave her the epidural. I woke up and the time was coming real fast and I was 10cm but my water still hadn't broken so my doctor had to break my water. He said ok Maria are you ready and they gave my mom her little suit and we were on our way. My mom was right there the whole time holding my hand and saying baby you can do it, baby just push and take slow deep breaths.

After my baby was born, my mom was able to walk her to the nursery with the little hat on her head. She didn't even let me and Billy name our own daughter, the name she gave her was so special and she has part of my name as well. She then called my dad and they told him over the radio that he was a proud grandfather of a baby girl. He put his riders out and came straight to the hospital where his daughter and new grandbaby was. My mom then called Billy and his family to tell them the good news. They came to the hospital to see us and could not believe how beautiful she was. She had a head full of hair and she looked just like me. She weighed six pounds and ten ounces and was perfect in my eyes. I could not believe that we had created a life. I was now responsible for another human being. That is a lot to digest as a teenager. I never thought that I could love another person so much.

That was a happy day for everyone. She was the first granddaughter in his family. Everyone else in his family had boys, so I knew that they would spoil her every chance they got. I was home schooled for a while after I had her. I had a good teacher who would bring my lessons to me so that I would not get too far behind. Now here is the catch I never met his family until the day I had our daughter, all they said is he always talked about a girl named Maria. His aunt came up there and she looked at me and smiled. She said now I finally get a chance to meet the young lady who had my nephew's nose open. The room was so packed and I was very tired. I needed some rest after all that and the nurse and doctor said that I needed some rest. Everybody started leaving and Billy kissed me on the lips and said I love you Maria for the first time. And the family that was in the room said now ain't that the cutest thing.

So they took our daughter back to her room and everybody was looking at her through the window. That night Billy stayed up there with us and our friends came a little later after everyone had left to congratulate us. I just knew he was going to stick around for us because he now had a little one to take care of. During that day when I had my baby, my brother had called from Florida and no one answered the phone so when they got home and they called him back. He was like where y'all been, mom told him at the hospital and he asked with who and what's wrong. Our mom said with your sister Maria she just had a baby girl by Billy and he was like what I'm going to kill that nigga, and there was silence for a while then she said he started to cry. He was like when did this happen and what she had and are they ok you mean to tell me mom she rode all the way to Florida with me and I didn't even know my baby sister was having a baby. And he cried worst and he was mad with me a long time until he came home to visit. When he saw us asleep in my room, all he could do was cry and leave the house. He just needed some time alone to himself so he went over to one of his girlfriend's house and told her the news. She was like what Maria ain't had no freaking baby and he called and I told her yes I did, and she asked if she could come over there to see us sometimes while my brother was home and I said sure. She said when she came out there that my brother was mad at me and he started crying again until he looked into her pretty, big brown eyes. She smiled at him, then he started crying even harder and he hugged me and said once she gets a little bit bigger I want you to come to Tampa to visit me. And so I took him up on the offer once she was six months old.

Billy would come to see us often in the beginning and I thought that was great because his family came out to our home as well to see the both of us. When I went back to school, his family kept her so that I could concentrate on my studies. I was so grateful for that. They were more than happy to help me in any way that they could. Unfortunately, when our daughter was two months old, he left us. He decided that he would be better off with someone else. The girl that he chose to be with almost took his life. She stabbed him, which put him in the hospital. Still, he thought that she was better than me. That was a hard pill to swallow because he was my first love and the father of my child. Then she tried to kill him again. I was there for him just like the first time because I still cared for him.

When he got well, we tried to rekindle our romance, but it was never the same. In the back of my mind, I always thought that he would get back with the other girl once she was released from jail. That is what prevented me from fully accepting him back into my heart.

Even though things with Billy and I did not work out, his family remained supportive of me and our daughter. They remained an active part of her life and they supported her in whatever she was involved in. I am eternally grateful for that. They have truly been a blessing to us. Even though I was young, I was proud to be a mother. Things got hard sometimes, but we made it through. I continued to go to school and I also worked part-time to support us. And even though I did it the wrong way, God did not condemn me. Even then, He was still in the midst, providing for me, comforting me, and guiding me. The hardest thing was when he started messing with my so called friend Shawna. He thought that was cool but it wasn't. We were no longer friends and I just gave up on Billy and me for good then. But we had a family business and everybody was selling except my mom and she wasn't having it. She really didn't know I was selling until she found it in my bag in my car. Yeah I had a car at the age 15 cause I was a mom, in school and finally graduated from progressive Christian Academy.   When summertime came up, it was on and popping. My dad had already taught me the game so I was true to it and not new to it. (Cause at first I didn't want to tell him what kind of business my family was in, because I didn't want him to rat us out so I said we are together so I'm going to tell him anyway. And I did it for years and I didn't have to worry about anything or any harm coming my way at all. ---Who are you talking about) When my daughter was six months old, I took that trip down south to see my brother., He was doing it up down there because he had met two guys that were from Macon and they went into business together.

They partied every day and I was like what the hell do they do when they have to go to work the next morning. I met this girl that was a good friend of my brother and I used to hang out with her. He had met this lady named Jean and she had a grown daughter who was away at school. Mannn, one night they got into it and I hid all the silverware. She must have been crazy to think she was going to hurt my brother. Then he met another chick who was a stripper and I already knew that wasn't going to last (she was a hoe) and I really didn't get up on her either. We would ride the strip at night and no guy would talk to me thinking my brother was my boyfriend. It was nice. We would ride around in his gold and black 280ZX then after two weeks I had to go back and we both cried when I left.

Growing Up as a Single Young Parent

After having my heart broken by Billy, I began to have self-esteem issues. I was not sure if I would find love again. Eventually, I recovered. I met a guy named Mark and we hit it off. At first, I didn't want to deal with him romantically, but I figured I didn't have anything to lose. He was a football star at the school that we attended and all the girls loved him.

His mom worked in the cafeteria at our school and his sister attended the school as well. They were very nice to me and we got along well. Mark was very protective of me. When my friends and I went out, he would act like our bodyguard. We went to the Georgia State Fair together, and everyone knew that we were a couple. Out of all the girls that he could have, he chose me. I felt like the luckiest girl alive.

I met a girl named Lisa. No one seemed to like her, but we became the best of friends. We were inseparable. If you saw me, you saw her, too. We trusted each other and tried not to do anything to hurt each other. We loved to shop at the Macon Mall, go out to eat, and to the Peacock Lounge and Mark would be right there with us, having a great time. Lisa would spend the night with me and we would stay up all night telling jokes until we fell asleep.

Eventually, Mark began to resent the amount of time Lisa and I spent together. I guess he was a little jealous. It became a major problem in our relationship. We began having arguments, which gradually became physical. He would jump on me and I would just sit there and cry. No one ever knew that he was abusing me because I am a private person. I would put on a happy face for the world and pretend that everything was alright.

I remember a time when Mark, Lisa, and I decided to go to the club. He got turned away because it was teen night and he was too old to get in. He got angry and insisted that I leave with him. When I refused, he tried to fight me right in front of Lisa. I begged her not to tell anyone about what had happened. In order to avoid a bigger scene, I decided to leave with him. I was so angry that I did not speak to him for the rest of the night because he had really pissed me off that night in front of my friend and the people at the door of the night club.

When my friends later asked me what happened, I told them that I was just tired and wanted to go home. Deep down, I wanted to just come clean and tell them all that had happened. I wanted to tell them that he was physically abusive and I was trying to prevent another beating.

In addition to the physical violence, he began to mistrust me. He thought that I was seeing other men. I don't know what made him think that. Everyone knew that we were together, so no one even tried to approach me in that way. Because I knew a lot of guys, he thought that I was trying to be a whore and things got much worse. If I didn't come to school, he thought that I had cut class to be with someone else. He would go to my house and wait until I got there. If I went somewhere with someone, he would try to have sex with me to see if it felt the same. I guess that was his way of checking to see if I had been with another guy. What began as protection became possession. I was no longer my own person, I belonged to him. I became terrified of him, but still I stayed with him. He was horrible to me and I kept it to myself. I didn't want people to know that I had a fool for a boyfriend.

Finally, I decided that enough was enough. I began walking home with a girl and her brother. He was interested in me and I liked him, too. Mark and I had stopped seeing each other and he had started a relationship with someone else. I explained that I had just gotten out of a relationship and that I was not interested in starting a new one just yet.

Mark and his new girlfriend made it known that they were together, and oddly enough, that bothered me. He did not treat me well, but I still wanted him back. Somehow, I missed having him in my life. I finally decided that I would do whatever I had to do to get him back.

One day in school, I decided that I would pretend that I was expecting a baby. I waited until his girlfriend and her friends were walking down the hall and I began to rub my belly. After they passed us, my friends and I began laughing. We were so immature back then. She went back to him and told him that I was having a baby, so he left her and got back with me. I was so happy. That night, we made love and there I was, having another child.

Once I had gone to the doctor and received confirmation that I was indeed pregnant, things got better between us. He began to treat me better, for a while, at least. He was at my house almost every day. He even asked my mother for my hand in marriage. She explained that he had to ask my father. He had already purchased the rings and everything. He asked my father, but my father was absolutely against it. He told Mark "Hell No" at first, but eventually he came around.

When I was about three months pregnant, all hell broke loose. A man in the military became interested in me. He was in the army with my uncle. He would call me and send me clothes and write me letters whenever he got the chance. He and my uncle were in the same branch. That is how we met. I explained everything to him about my relationship with Mark. He said that he was okay with that. Even though this guy was a better man, I stayed with Mark like a fool. One day, I stopped to talk to him. Before I knew it, Mark was driving down the street. When he saw me, he called me, but I didn't respond. That made him furious. He jumped out of the car and grabbed me by my arm. I began to cry and he hit me. By this time, the other guy came off of the porch and confronted Mark. He told me to get on the porch and let him handle the situation.

Still I stayed with Mark. One day I cut school to go to court with Mark. On the way there, my left eye began to twitch. No matter what I tried, it would not stop. By ten o'clock, it finally stopped. That night, as we walked down the street, we saw my mom crying. I asked her what was wrong and she informed me that my father had been shot and killed. That was the worst second day of my life. He died on my daughter's second birthday. I am glad that she was too young to know what was happening. I had lost my daddy and he was gone forever. We called my brother in Florida and he came right away.

I was so distraught that I even tried to kill my baby. My mother took me to the doctor and explained what had happened. He expressed his sympathy and prescribed some medication to calm me down. I went into a deep sleep right there in the doctor office. When I awoke, my mother took me to Jones County to visit my dad's sister and the rest of the family. When she came to the door and looked at me she begin to cry saying I looked just like my dad, which caused me to break down. My family had to calm me down all over again.

By this time, I was eight months pregnant. And they were doing an investigation into his murder. They were saying that maybe it was a hit from the mob, because my dad was into the dope game real hard and they couldn't find the man at first. My oldest brother didn't even come to the funeral. He was out looking for the person who killed our dad and I was real scared for him because he was the type that would shoot you and ask no questions later.

On the day we buried him, many of my classmates and teachers came to show their support. They showed me a lot of love during my time of sorrow. Those who could not attend expressed their sympathy when I returned to school. They really supported me when I needed it the most.

A month later, it was time for homecoming and I was determined to go. It was a time when I had the chance to see family members that I don't often see. My doctor told me not to go too far from home because the baby was due any day. That Friday I went to the mall to get an outfit so that I would look cute for homecoming. The next morning, we left for homecoming. We went to the parade and I began to have labor pains. I didn't tell anyone because I really wanted to see my family. After the parade, the pain got more intense. We went out to eat and I excused myself to use the restroom. I thought that I was going to have the baby right there in the bathroom. I ran out to tell my family and they rushed me to the hospital. When I arrived, they took me right away. My doctor told my fast tail not to go too far from home, but a hard head makes a soft behind. I thought the doctors there were preparing me for delivery. Instead, one doctor came out to tell me that they do not deliver babies. After I screamed at him, he apologized and suggested that I go back to the hospital in Bibb County so they put me in the ambulance and one of my family members was in the back with me while the others followed on the interstate. They moved fast. When I arrived at the hospital, it was time to have the baby. There was no time for them to give me any pain medication. They rolled me down the hall and suddenly, my baby was on his way out. They got me into the room just in time. I had a five pound, five ounce baby boy. To make it even better, he was born on my father's birthday. That moment was bittersweet because I didn't know whether to laugh or cry. I was happy about my son's birth, but at the same time, I was sad because my father wasn't there to meet him.

Sadly, the man who killed my father was still at large. That kept me in constant fear. For an entire year, I was under police protection because I was told that he wanted to kill me, too. I am not sure why he wanted me dead, but that didn't even matter. I just wanted to pick up the pieces of my life and move on. Life without him was so empty. And on top of that, he wanted my life. He was finally arrested when I was a junior in high school. He was sentenced to life in jail without the possibility of parole. But when it was time for him to go to court and get his sentence, my family would not allow me go so therefore they told me what the sentence was instead.

After my father died, my relationship with Mark was never the same. My mom told him that he was no longer welcomed at my house, so he left. When he came back, Billy had stopped by to see our daughter. Mark lost it. He broke my mother's window and it was an ugly scene. I called the police and he was permanently banned from coming to our house.

My brother took our father's death pretty hard as well. He dropped out of school and moved back to Georgia to be with us. I was happy to have him back home. He found a good job with CDI and we began to rebuild our relationship.

Mark was in and out of my life, so I had to make the hard decision to really let him go. His jealousy was unbearable and I was sick and tired of it. I had to finally say, "Enough is enough." When sorrow and tears far outweigh joy and laughter, it is time to let it go. I had to realize that misery was not what God had ordained for my life. Because Mark used to beat me so much and I was so scared of him that he use to beat me in front of his family that's just how bad it was, and they wouldn't say a word at all. We had some good times and a lot of bad times. And the guy from the military wasn't hearing that he was still jumping on me so I had to do what I had to do.

Going Through the Motions of Loving a Man

Just when I thought I had gotten Mark out of my system, what did I do? I let him back into my life. We started dealing with each other again, because I just couldn't seem to love me more than I loved him. He was involved in a bad car accident and I felt sorry for him. I even accompanied him to his doctor's appointments. After his accident, he decided to drop out of school. Before long, I was expecting another baby and Mark was not too thrilled about having another child on the way. We were already having problems and this news didn't help matters. I would spend the night at his house and he would go out and leave me there. Sometimes he didn't even bother to come home. I would get up in the middle of the night and pace the floor, wondering where he was and who he was with. I would tell myself that he would be back sooner or later so that I could go back to bed. (But that didn't work and I was still up looking like a fool).

Before I knew it, it was morning and he still had not arrived home. I called his cell phone and another woman answered. When I asked where he was, she told me that he was asleep. I even asked her to wake him up to let him know that I was on the line. I felt so foolish talking on the phone to my boyfriend's mistress. (NOW I FELT SO LOW THAT MORNING)

When he finally made it home, we began to argue and he beat me up. His mom tried to stop him and he told her to stay out of his way. I didn't go around my family for a while because I didn't want them to see what he had done to me because he had swelled my lip up and he was like an inch away from hitting my head with a baseball bat. Boy was I scared. I saw my life flash in front of my eyes that day.

Things finally got so bad that I moved back home. I had lost every ounce of joy that I had left. I decided that I had to let go of him or I could lose my life. Whenever anybody made him mad he would come to me talking about it and if I didn't have the right answer he would beat my ass for no reason at all. He was crazy. If I didn't cry the first time he hit me, he would get mad and hit me even harder till I cried. I left and never looked back. Then I found out that I was pregnant again. I just couldn't seem to be rid of that man! I was like oh gosh what is wrong with me. I didn't want another baby by this man.

Even though I was pregnant, I tried to move on with my life. I met a man named June and he stole my heart. I explained the entire situation to him and he understood. He was even alright with the fact that I was pregnant with another man's child. He said that he would not put any pressure on me. He allowed me to set the pace of the relationship. That meant so much to me. He allowed me to have more control than I ever had with Mark. I decided to move into an apartment in the projects. I wanted to try to be on my own. He would come to check on me quite often. Boy was that a trip my mom didn't like him either so when he and his friends came over everybody ran and hid in closets and rooms. One weekend, I decided to spend the night with my mother. I developed a sore throat, so I figured some hot tea would make me feel better. I went to bed early that night. The next morning, I woke up with severe abdominal pains. My mother called 911. When they arrived, they took me directly to the hospital. That day, I gave birth to another son. He had stopped breathing, but they were finally able to get him to breathe on his own. Finally, I heard him cry. I was relieved to hear that strong cry. Then it happened. He was placed in ICU. He had started to decline. I had to go to my room without him. I began to pray for the both of us. The doctors told me that his prognosis was not good and that I would have to go home without him. He had bleeding on his brain and they were not sure if he would pull through.

When I got home, June came to see me. I told him about the baby. He tried his best to console me. I went to the hospital every day to see him. I really believed that he would be alright. Then one day he got worse. The hospital tried to reach me, but I was not available. I finally got the news around 2:00 PM that my son had died that morning at 11:00 AM. I went crazy. I hopped in the car and went straight to the hospital. I called Mark and he came to the hospital, too. All I could do was cry. I cried until there were no tears left. They took us to the room where our son was. They had dressed him and placed him in a basket. He looked like he was sleeping. I sat in a chair and held him close to me, rocking gently back and forth.

That was the first time I had the chance to hold him in my arms. To make matters worse, Mark decided to pick the baby's arm up and let it fall several times. I became enraged. I could not believe that he was doing that. It was bad enough that I lost him. But for him to do that only added insult to injury. I began to cry once again. Before we left, the hospital took pictures of him and gave us copies to take with us.

By this time, I felt like God had forgotten about me. He had taken my son away from me before I could even hold him. I had the daunting task of arranging a funeral for my son. My pastor put together a graveside service. My uncle bought him a suit, and my aunt helped me buy the casket. I cried through the entire process. The pain I felt was indescribable. Mark didn't even show up at his own son's funeral. The graveside service went as well as it could. I went up to his casket and held him one last time. All I could do was ask God why I had to go through so much loss, pain, and suffering. He was buried right above my father's head. It still hurt as I think of my son, he would have turned 17 years old this year if he had lived. He was a month old when he died which was on Father's Day 1993.

When I got home, I needed time to get myself together. So, I thanked everyone for their support and asked if I could be left alone for a while. Later, June came over and comforted me. He assured me that everything would be alright. I told him that he could never understand what I was going through. He had never experienced loss like I had. He still stuck by me, consoling me until I fell asleep. Later, June and I got very close. He moved in with me after a while, but he still respected my wishes to take things slow. Almost a year had passed before we even became intimate. He treated me like a queen at all times, and I really loved him for that. He loved my children like they were his own flesh and blood. He filled the void that had formed inside of me long ago.

Just When My Life Couldn't Get Worse

Just when I thought my fairytale life had begun, the other shoe dropped. I found out that he had a girlfriend and that they had a child together. All the time we were together, he made me believe that he was completely unattached and baggage-free. I fell hard for him, too. When we finally did become intimate, I found myself pregnant after the first time. I went to the doctor, and sure enough, I was having his baby. I was still trying to heal from losing my son, so I had mixed feelings about this pregnancy. I went home and cried. I thought, "This can't be happening to me!" I was upset because I was pregnant by someone else's man. The man I thought really honored and cherished me.

My whole world was turned upside down. I called my friend for advice. She assured me that it would all work out and that he would be a good father to our baby. We were living together and baby mama drama began to surface. I tried not to let it bother me because I loved the ground he walked on. Then I started to hear rumors that he was seeing other women around town. I found myself pulling him out of other women's houses. He even tried to sleep with women that I knew personally. That really pissed me off. My mother did not approve of him at all. She always thought that he was up to no good. My brothers hated him because they knew that he was not treating me right.

This once gentleman became violent and abusive. This was in addition to all of his cheating and lying. I turned a blind eye to it all because I wanted so desperately to be with him. When I was five months pregnant, I tried to pull him out of yet another woman's house. Like a fool, I left empty-handed. He refused to come out. I found myself going through his wallet and beeper, calling the numbers that I found. They would tell him and he would come home and fight me. It was a vicious cycle. When I was seven months pregnant, I went to another one of his girlfriend's house and we talked for about two hours. He got mad about that, but I didn't care. He even began to have an affair with my son's godmother. That really tore me up inside. They began sneaking around and people began to talk. One night, I had some friends over. They decided to put in an adult movie. Who did I see on the tape? It was my so-called-man getting busy with a white woman. I felt like a fool. I had just been humiliated in front of a group of my closest friends. I just got up cried and went to bed.

Stress and drama caused me to be sick for the remainder of my pregnancy. Then one day, I slipped and fell and had to go to the hospital. He didn't show up until it was time for me to be released. After the fall, I couldn't seem to get well, so I was placed on bed rest at the hospital until it was time for me to have the baby. Every day for three weeks, he and my mom came to sit with me. I also had to undergo stress tests on a daily basis. On February 14th, I gave birth to my last son at 7:30 PM. I had him in the bed before the doctors could even get prepared. He had to be taken to the ICU and I was in a wheelchair right behind them. I could not believe that I had had another sick baby (I said lawd why is this happening to me). He was a strong baby and he pulled through. After three weeks, he came home. He was small, but healthy. My cousin decided to take him back to the country with her and I agreed. Two months later, I didn't even recognize him. He was such a fat baby! I had to ask her who he was. She happily shouted, "He's your baby, silly!" Thank you Lord for bestowing grace and mercy on my son. I guess God really does know just how much you can bear. Losing another child would have certainly killed me.

How do I begin to explain the hardest part of my life? I stayed with June a while longer and allowed myself to put up with his other girlfriend and he had a so-called ex-wife who stayed in and out of prison, and every time she got out she came looking for June. Times got hard and I was evicted from my apartment. I then moved in with him and his girlfriend (I know what y'all saying and looking like I had it like that no freaky shit now). Yes, you read correctly. I moved in with them. She had never met me and was under the impression that I was his cousin. I allowed him to take me to work and drop me off, while he used my car all day. I was really a fool when it came to him. No one could tell me anything when it came to him. To me, he could do no wrong. People would tell me that he was riding around town in my car with other women while I was at work.

One day, he even had the nerve to ask if I would have a threesome with him and his girlfriend. I let him know that he had the wrong sister on that one. I also told him that it was nasty and wrong of him to even come to me with such a proposition. There are certain things that you don't even do or say to someone you claim to love. After some time had passed, I moved back in with my mom. We parted ways for a spell, but once again, I let him back into my life. Once again he caused me much heartache. I found myself living with him and his girlfriend again because my mother was being too hard on me. She really was telling me right, but I couldn't see it at the time. One day, he got jumped and his girlfriend and Jumped in the car to see about him. We all met at the hospital and found that he was past the legal alcohol limit. We went back to the house and I had already planned what I would say to him in the morning. I must have gone overboard, because before I knew it, we were fighting like cats and dogs. I told him to take me to my mother's house and his girlfriend wondered why we were arguing. I finally told her that he was the father of my youngest child.

Back then, I cursed like a sailor and spoke my mind without worrying how you felt about it. If you kept pushing me, I would fight until I saw blood. Thank God for changing me. He made me so mad that I went to a payphone and told them that he was holding his family against their will. Before I knew it, they had the place surrounded. Boy, was that a mess!

We decided to go our separate ways once again. For a while, I refused to speak to him. He would call me and beg me to come back to him. Then, he decided to tell his girlfriend that our son was not his. That hurt me to my heart. All I could do was cry like a big baby. (I WAS LIKE THAT BITCH)

Eventually we began to talk again over the phone. He and his girlfriend had moved into a house in Bloomfield. There I was again, running after him. One day, they had a cookout and she took our son inside. She looked inside his mouth and realized that I was telling the truth about my son. She stormed out of that house like a ball of fire. She told him, "You lied to me! He is your son!!!" Apparently, she could tell by his teeth that he was the father. That night, they were in a terrible fight. She begged me to call the police on him. I didn't want to, but I did as she asked. I tried to warn him that the police were on their way. I begged him to leave immediately, but he refused. When the police arrived, he was arrested and taken to jail. She and I began to cry and walked back into the house.

After his arrest, his girlfriend moved on fairly quickly. That wasn't my business, so I left it alone. His mom and I would go visit him on Sundays. I told him that I would not leave his side. One Sunday I decided to let him know that his girlfriend had moved on. I guess it really hurt him because he cried. He probably never thought that Karma would come back around on him.

One night his mother told me that I should move back with my mother while he was incarcerated. I called my mom, and she welcomed me and my children back with open arms. She wondered what had taken me so long to reach out to her. I continued to visit him and one day he popped the question. He asked me if I loved him. I told him that I did. He showed me a tattoo on his arm with our names on it. I began to cry and so did he. He asked me to marry him and I accepted. We blew a kiss through the glass window and said our goodbyes.

He called me collect so much that our phone got disconnected. I would then just go to another telephone company and start all over again. I continued to visit him until they transferred him to a mini prison camp. I was only able to see him about three times during those eight months. That was okay because we needed some time apart.

One weekend, my mom went out of town and the lights got turned off. It was very cold at that time and I didn't know what to do. His mom would come get us, but she didn't know that we were in the dark. One cold night, she told me that she was on her way and that I should be ready when she arrived. I believe that we really became close during that time. We formed a friendship. She asked me if I wanted to marry her son. I informed her that I had every intention of marrying him. I loved him with all that I had. I just prayed that he had changed his ways. That time had run out and I was tired of staying with her too and I went back to my mom's house where there were rules that weren't made to be broken. and I really enjoyed staying with my friend it was me and the kids and I still talked to my mom a lot but we just couldn't stay together though I loved her with all my might. I was still doing hair, I had been braiding for years and I wasn't looking for another man right then, cause mine was in jail but I knew I needed and wanted sex too (I'm just keeping it real with you). We used to go to this club called Grants Lounge that was downtown Macon, everyone was down there every weekend and week day just partying their behinds off.

Later, I moved in with a female friend of mine. We would hang out together all the time. One night while we were out, I met a police officer. He was fine like hell and he was just what I was looking for at the right time and plus I wasn't really looking for nobody. It just happened. We were talking outside the club and my friend was getting mad cause she wanted to talk to him. She was tall, fat and ugly with some missing teeth (no man wouldn't mind that). He asked what were we about to do and I said we are going to the waffle house on Spring Street how could he not notice me, cute in the face, small in the waist and fine with a big juicy booty. I was a fine chick but without the nasty image. We all sat down and ate and we left and he called me. Yeah baby, he was interested in me and I didn't resist. My man was still incarcerated, and I was in desperate need of some TLC. We went to his house and he turned me every which way but loose. It was the best sex I had ever had. He took me home that night and I never called him back. Men do it all the time, so why shouldn't we? Whenever he saw my friend, he would ask about me. She never gave him any details. And all I could do was think about that officer he worked for the Macon police department and his name was Craig. I loved me some Craig and he made me feel good and like I was on cloud 1000 that night was the bomb. He licked my forbidden place and he just made love to me like no other.

June was scheduled to be released just before Christmas. His mother and I went to pick him up. We stayed with his mother until we could get our own place. Everything was going well until

I ran into that cop. I didn't know what to expect, but he never said a word. After that, June and I started selling drugs together and we became all about making that money. We thought we were unstoppable and when I did see the cop I wanted to say something to him but I was scared to say anything.

When I First Took Sick

In 1999, while I was working at a local department store that had just opened up and I was taking class's downtown as well, I began to experience a stabbing pain in my lower abdomen. I couldn't figure out why, so I went to the doctor to check it out. He ran some tests and told me that he would call me with the results. He called me two weeks later while I was in class and he asked me did I have the time to sit down and talk to me so I told him to let me call him back, and that I needed to go and talk to my teacher for a minute. I go in and tell her that I needed somewhere to go in private so I could talk to my doctor and he informed me that I had cancer. I wanted to scream at the top of my lungs at that moment. They told me to come in as soon as possible. He examined me and confirmed that I had cancerous cells growing in my private area and all I could do was cry like a baby. He needed some more info and I had to get lab work done and make an appointment to come in and have the operation done in his office. I was really scared so I went home and told my husband (yeah we had gotten married June 12, 1998). I had to drop of school and I had to quit my job that I loved so well.

They performed laser surgery to remove the cancerous cells. At first he only saw two big cells. Then he later found four more cells. All I could do was cry out to God for grace and mercy. I had to stop working because I had lost my will to do anything. God was there with me through it all. I can now say that I am a cancer survivor. PRAISE THE LORD! I have been cancer-free for eleven years now. God is truly my healer.

In 2000, I began to develop severe headaches. I had to take my children to the optometrist for an annual exam. My daughter needed glasses and I wanted some too. They looked so cute on her and we looked just alike so I wanted some to). When the doctor examined me, he found fluid behind my eyes. Eventually I had to have a spinal tap and get on medication. I did not enjoy that one bit! They asked me to decide what I wanted to do. They told me two ways that they had to do the operation. One was to help my vision, they would operate on my eyes, then the second one was to put a shunt in my brain, I told them that I needed time to think things over. My headaches got so bad that I called them back the following Monday.

In January 2000, I had my first brain surgery. I was in the ICU for three days. My children were too young to even come see me in there. When I did go home, I got an infection and had to go right back to the hospital. I was there for a week. When I went back home, I became even more ill. By February, I was back in the hospital. This time I was there for almost a month. Around that time, I began to use drugs. I wanted to lose weight. My husband was a dope dealer at the time and he fed the drugs to me. And when I say drugs, I mean crack cocaine. I was in and out of the hospital and they drew my blood often. I am not sure if they ever detected it in my system. So it all started at my mom's house. We were living on Lowe Street so I told him the only way I would try is if he tried too. When he tried, we did it like five hours and my head was hurting so bad because we had not eaten anything that whole day. When you do drugs, it makes you not want food but water or any liquids will do the trip because your mouth be dry as cotton. Then I knew I had to go to work and I didn't want to go because I was high. I wanted more but I knew I had to be to work in one hour, so I called in and told them that I would be a little late and she said ok. So there I was getting even higher and when he would go down stairs I would steal me one. Hey he was a dope dealer so he could get more. He had turned me into someone else that I didn't like at all. I went into work. Now take in mind, you have to read the gas pumps and record them and I forgot to do that. I was high so I wasn't thinking of that. I went on to work as usual and my kids and my ex came in and bought something and gave me the change. This guy we both knew was trying to steal something out the store and I looked him in the eyes and said not on my watch now get the fuck out my store before I call the damn police and he left. So the same night another worker called in and said she was going to be late as well and I said ok but hurry up because my ride was there to get me. Now remember I didn't even read the pump from my shift. I said oh well time to go get messed up again. I didn't have to work the next day so it was like party over here party over there. When she did come in, like after one hour, I was mad as hell so I gave her my paper work and I went home(and got high).The next day when I go in to get my check, the manager called me in the back and she asked me what time did I come in yesterday and I told her like twenty minutes after my scheduled time and she was like ok then. Then she said we got another major problem and I was like what's wrong. She said my register didn't add up on the money nor the pump (I know what y'all thinking I stole money) well to answer her question I was like I was running behind time and I totally forgot to read the pumps. I went straight to work and I said how sorry I was as well. Then she said we have a bigger issue and I was like (what the fuck now) was this pick on or fuck up Maria's day or what?? Then she said the most hurting thing out her mouth that I was on camera putting money in my pocket. I was like my family came up here and purchase some things and they gave me the money that was left over for some lunch. But she wasn't hearing that and at the same time while I was writing my statement about what I had just told her. Someone had called the police. My ex had called up there to see if I was ready and they told him a lie that I had left. He went on about his business so they told me that I could wait outside. And as I was waiting on his mom, guess who pulls up, the motherfucking police and they locked my ass up. His mom was across the street paying on her car payment and she hurried across the street to see what was going on. So I told her to call her son and my folks to get me out of jail. Y'all know I was mad as hell … just got paid and couldn't do shit.

My family had to come and bail me out of jail. I was mad like hell with them white folks, because I had done nothing for them to treat me like they did, I had lost my job but I didn't give a darn so I told them that I was going to sue the hell out of them. I went to court about a month later and they found me not guilty cause they had found out that someone else, (the managers, had been stealing the money and putting the blame on the other workers. They were arrested and charged with theft by taken in the 1st degree. Boy was I happy and they offered me my job back so I went back to work because I needed the money to support my habit. So things got worse as soon as I went back to work, we were evicted and they came and got our van so therefore we had to go live with his parents once again, and we had to come up with a good lie to tell as to why we lost our apartment and van in the same week. Not ain't that something, we had to come up with a lie for my family as well as our kids.

One night, he woke me up with crack on a beer bottle. He told me to smoke it. We did it all night long. When the sun came up, we were still at it. I was so weak that all I wanted to do was sleep. I got even sicker. I thought that I was going to die. I ended up back in the hospital with another infection. This time, they didn't let me go home. I was in there on my birthday and I was mean to everyone who crossed my path. And they had the kitchen to bake me a cake and I still wasn't hearing that mess from nobody and I gave everybody my ass to kiss on that day.

In the ICU, my children could not visit and I became very depressed. After I was released, I had to go in for a checkup because I was unable to keep anything down. He told me that I needed to go back to the hospital and I had a fit. I was tired of being admitted to the hospital. He told me that he would have me arrested if I did not go. Needless to say, I went voluntarily. My drug use got even worse after this last admission. Somehow, people were unaware of my drug problem. Within a month of my release from the hospital, I thought I was doing well. Suddenly, I couldn't eat or drink. My weight plummeted from 225 to 129 pounds in less than six months. My life seemed to be spiraling out of control. One day I felt something pop inside of me. I would later find out that a cyst had burst. This happened after my neighbors refused to take me to the hospital. They felt really guilty about that.

I was immediately taken to the OR. Cysts were popping up along every angle. The doctor said that I had died four or five times during the operation, but he refused to give up on me. I remember seeing an image at the end of a tunnel. It looked like a tall person holding something small in his arms. I thought it was my daddy holding my son that had passed away. I also heard a voice telling me that it was not yet my time to go. I still had work to do here on Earth. My husband recalled them rushing down the hall reciting a Code Blue. He realized that they were talking about me and quickly moved our children to another room before they could see him crying. I was in the ICU for three weeks. I could not get out of bed and my body was full of tubes. They had me on so much medication that all I did was sleep. One day the meds wore off and I was up when the nurse came in. What I saw horrified me. I could see the inside of my belly! Everyone came running because they thought that something bad had happened to me.

I had a feeding tube in me for a long time. One day, they tried to take it out to allow me to drink. I got so sick that they had to reinsert the tube. I remember prayer warriors from my church coming to pray for me. Everyone cried because I was crying. I couldn't even see my children during that time. I stayed for three weeks so that the infection could drain out. After that, I had another operation. I had been stuck so many times that my arms were severely bruised. My doctor was furious. When the operation was over, they put me in a private room and I was as big as Texas. I had retained a lot of fluid from the operation. I had to learn how to walk all over again. The doctor ordered a bedside commode for me and I got stuck on it! I cried and went to sleep right there. I must have been there for thirty to forty-five minutes. After one week I was released. People came by to cook for us every day. They helped me with the children and allowed me to get plenty of rest. I had to have my meds every thirty minutes to an hour that he had to quit his job. Soon my husband began to feed me crack again even though I had medicine going into me through the I.V. He made me feel like he didn't care about me at all. Sometimes he would leave the house in the middle of the night and get drugs. He would then feed it to me along with my scheduled medication. I was too weak to even refuse. One night he got ready to give me my medication, and my I.V. line got stuck.

He couldn't flush it. If he didn't get it right, I would have to be readmitted to the hospital. That was the last thing I wanted. We had just done some drugs about two hours prior to that so this was not an option. Finally, he was able to flush the line. He gave me my meds and I went to sleep.

When things began to return to normal, he began cheating on me again. I could not stand it. When he went to the hospital, I cheated on him with his best friend. I didn't even care if he found out about it. I was fed up. Eventually, I lost the house because I refused to pay the bills. My drug habit had gotten worse and I began to look awful. I did not care about anyone or anything.

I finally had to check into a drug treatment center. I did very well in treatment and I had enrolled in college. I was finally on the right track. I was so proud of myself. I finally left my husband alone, never to return. I joined a support group and met a lot of good people there. They encouraged me and I thanked them for that.

The old ways have passed away because God saw fit to save me. Despite all of the things I have done, I am still here. If you want God to change your life, you must first go to Him with an honest and sincere heart. Once you give God your burdens, stop trying to carry them and take them back. He's got it all under control. If you have faith the size of a mustard seed, God will multiply it. I had the faith to believe that I would defeat that drug demon and I am here today . . . . Conqueror. I am stronger because God called me friend, daughter, worthy. Will you answer His call?

AThinLineBetweenLifeand Death (Going Through Hell)

I was still very sick and I use to think that all hell was breaking loose around me. And I knew better but at the time I really didn't care about nothing. My heart was getting very cold towards people. Well I was having so many problems I didn't know how to deal with it. I began to ask myself, where do I begin from here? After my first operation on my head because I was dying on the inside and the doctor was like I could have my eyes operated on for my vision or I could get the shunt for everything. And after the first one it only lasted for about one month it had to come out I guess because I went outside to soon. Then I was back in the hospital again and they said that they had to remove it, because the other end was in my belly. Then I was like God, why all of this is happening to me? Then I was there for one week. June was there every day... him and our kids and my mom sometimes. People used to come and see me and we would talk until I was tired and I needed my rest. During that first time, I was so weak cause I was doing drugs too (ok I'm keeping it real with my readers). I wasn't happy at all. I had a man who didn't give a damn about me cause if he did, he wouldn't been feeding the drugs to me (crack that is).

He claimed he loved me. Yeah right so when I first tried crack it was so good that I didn't want to stop but I had to, because I had to be to work that same day and I was like damn. (I went to work with a bad headache because I haven't eaten anything and I didn't know what to do, so he (my ex-husband) and the kids came where I was working at a store. I gave them some money after they had bought something but at the same time this guy I knew was trying to steal something out the store. so I went on with my shift and the lady who was to come in after me said that she was running behind and could I cover for her, and I said yes but what I forgot to do was go outside and read the gas pumps and everything else. So I went on home after she finally came in and I was so tired cause what had happened before I went to work, then I stopped and reported to work not feeling well at all. so the next day came and I didn't anything and o went to work and the drawer had been short the night before they thought I had got the money and when my shift was over I noticed that something was really wrong. and I didn't think of nothing about it at all so they let me off early so I asked could I call my ride and they gave me some kind of excuse as to why I could not use the phone.

I went outside to call him from the pay phone and as I was waiting on him I saw his mom across the street at the car lot I waved at her to let her know I was ready then ten minutes later the cops came to the store and we spoke and everything. then they went in and talk with the boss and they came out and walked up to me and said can I speak to you for a minute and I said yes, not knowing that they were about to arrest me for something I had no control over they lead me to the back office and the boss jumped all on my case about the money that was missing, and I explained everything to her that had just happened the night before the other lady called up there and they asked her did she come in one hour later and do you know what that bitch said, no she was on time for her shift. and then they told me to write a statement of everything I had just told them and my boss said she was pressing charges against me and she wanted me locked up and that's what they did and soon as they were walking me to the patrol car my ex-mother came over and I told her to call my mom and her son cause I didn't know what was going on. And they took me to jail and I was like it ain't no getting better for me that night and my mom then came down to get me and I was charged with theft by taking. I was mad as hell and they said that I wasn't allowed at their store anymore so the next day I sent my ex-husband there to pick up my check, and I went and got it cashed and went and got high that night all the night long till it wasn't no more money.

I felt like a fool the next day when my kids needed money for school and the night before that we were on our way home from picking up crack and as we were pulling into the apartment that we had in the Peach Orchard he had just put music on in our van and they were there to repo our van, and the guy didn't let us get the music nor the radio, he had said whatever was attached in there belonged in the van. So we felt quite dumb that night and we went on inside the house and got high. So a few weeks later we got put out our apartment because we weren't paying our rent because of the drug use. then we had come up with a lie to tell our parents as to why we moved and I felt so bad, cause my kids really didn't have no place to live. So his mom told us that we could come around there to live with them (she too stayed in the peach orchard) so there we were staying with her and they didn't know anything about our drug use.

He and I went back to work and we were back in our own place again. We moved into this big ole house on the south side of town. One of his friends was renting out houses and apartments and we really wanted that house. We knew we had to get our act together if we wanted it.

About a month after we moved in, my social security came in and they wrote me a check for six thousand dollars. I was like yeah it's getting high time for us. When I got my money, my daughter and I went on a shopping spree and I didn't tell a soul but then I thought to tell June what was going on and why we were gone so long. We got high that night like we had won the lottery. I wasn't even thinking about getting the most important thing which was a refrigerator to put our food in to keep it from spoiling. I went out and bought a lot of stuff for the house and my kids said that they wanted to go on a trip, so we were supposed go to this theme park but it wasn't in season yet. So we went to Tybee Island. The family and three of their closest friends went with us and it took forever getting there. We went through different cities and the white folks didn't like blacks (and I said what the fuck). Once again it was the same thing and I was like we will wait until we get where we are going before we eat and I knew that everyone was tired too. We were going over these tall bridges, over all this water I was like I can swim but darn this is a lot of water to drink, then finally we were at our stop and I was like bout time, my butt was beginning to hurt. We went on the strip and were trying to find somewhere to park. We had to pay $20 for both cars. That was okay because I had the money. I told them that everything was on me, so we found someplace to eat and had breakfast. We talked for a while and I said we all got to get something to get in the water with, and we did and I bought my brother a pair of sunglasses that was 20 dollars. It didn't matter the cost cause that was my brother. We had that brother and sister love. He was in a wheel chair then and we had to push him across the sand. He said he wanted to sit on the dock. I said that nigga wasn't slick. He wanted to sit and watch women all day. He saw big and little fat butts all day and I looked back at him and I said look at my big brother. But as long as everyone was enjoying themselves, that was all good. We stayed there for hours. It was so hot it felt like an oven t outside, so the kids played so hard all I could do is laugh at everyone. Our mom stayed up there with my brother. I was in the water the whole day and my body was tired. I looked around and I was like who are those people on the bridge sleep. He must had said those are our kids up there sleeping with their mouths open and I was laughing so hard l my belly hurt. It was beginning to get dark and cold so I said load them up and moved them out. We all took showers on the beach and washed our hair and we were on the road to coming back home.

I could not drive because I was so tired and wanted to go to sleep. I had tried to drive but I was going in and out the traffic so someone else had to drive the rental car. We got home real late and everyone stayed with us that night. We all slept like some happy babies and I wasn't going to get high while they were there with us, so I waited till the next night and we did the damn thing. My mom was having some problems with her then hubby and we went to see a root worker; now take in mind that we were going to church and we knew better but I don't know what the problem was with us. We go see this man and he was telling us all this crazy stuff and was telling us these things to do to get this man out my mom's life. This same week we were having family day and my family lead the early morning devotion and it just didn't feel right, because our pastor walked out as we got ready to lead the devotion. He never had done that before. At the end, I was like service today wasn't right. I felt like he had a vision or something of us going to a root worker or something and I really didn't care I just wanted this man out our lives. It was what it was and I felt like it had worked cause he left the house for a while and we were back to being a happy family again. Then I got word of this other pastor in Macon who was a root worker too and he asked us to bring certain things to him, I left my churchman, went to his church and gave it to one of his members and I left and went and got high.

Things started getting worse and my drug use got real bad. We had to move again and we went back to his mom's house once again and was really feeling like shit. The checks kept rolling in at the same time so the total at the end was $20,000.00. It got to the point that wherever we moved to, it just got worst and we started smoking with other people. He met some woman and we started going to her house smoking and I would give the dope dealer and his worker my EBT card. I even went as far as loaning out my mom's car, my car, he was sleeping with women and going under other people names... I didn't care I had to get my crack. Then he met this young girl and I had her do the crack. I did a lot of things that I wasn't feeling good about then I was caught and I had to go a drug treatment.

Then at the end I was giving another chance at life. I moved to Atlanta, GA and I joined a family church whom I love for life. Through a very dear friend that's how I met my soon to be husband. I told him everything I did in my life and he told me of his past and now we are getting married next year Glory be to God!!!!!!!

(AND AS I CLOSE I WANT TO SEND A SPECIAL THANKS TO THE DOCTORS FOR SEEING ABOUT ME AND THEY ARE AS FOLLOWINGS: DR CHRIS HENDRY FOR THE TIME AND TIMES YOU CARED FOR ME AND TO MAKE SURE MY HEALTH WAS GETTING BETTER, DR. LAWERENCE HARTMAN WHEN I FIRST CAME TO YOU WITH THE SERIOUS HEALTH PROBLEMS I WAS HAVING, AND YOU SAT ME DOWN AND EXPLAINED THE PROBLEMS AND TALK IT OVER ABOUT WHAT YOU WERE GOING TO DO. AND THE CALDWELL AND SON'S EYE FOR THE EYE EXAM AND FINDING THE PROBLEM BEFORE IT GOT WORST, AND DR FREEMAN FOR MANY AND MANY OF DAYS WHEN I WANTED TO GIVE UP AND YOU WOULDNT ALLOW IT AND FOR ALSO THE TEST AND EYE EXAMS THAT YOU GAVE ME. AND LAST BUT NOT THE LEAST THE MCCG STAFF THAT TOOK CARE OF ME WHEN I WAS SICK AND GOING THROUGH THE DIFFERENT OPERATIONS IT'S TOO MANY TO NAME GOD BLESS YOU ALL REAL GOOD!!!!!)

My Testimonial and Life Skill Lesson

Through it all, God has never left my side. I walked away from Him too many times to count, but He still remained faithful. For that reason, I will serve Him until I leave here. Thank you, Father, for believing in me when I didn't love or believe in myself. I have been through many storms in my life and I have learned many lessons. I must admit that many of my storms were self-created but God provided a way of escape each time. That is why I am the God-fearing woman I am today. The fact is, I should have been gone a long time ago. But, God saw fit that I should live and not die.

The trials of this life enable me to both learn from them and help someone else along the way. I spent many years running from my problems and running into trouble. The God I serve has blessed me through it all. My family has stuck by me through thick and thin. I graduated from college in 2006 when people doubted that I could even make it. I completed my drug treatment in 2006 as well. I was also blessed to receive a grant that allowed me to travel with the same center that ministered to me. I got a place of my own, a divorce, and a fresh start. I had learned to let go and let God have His way in my life. I now have a better relationship with my children. My daughter graduated in 2007. My mother's graduation present to her was a trip for two to Jamaica and the Cayman Islands. We had such a great time together.

When we returned, I moved to Atlanta and my life has definitely been looking up. God is taking me higher now that I have allowed Him to do His work in me and through me. My sons are happy and healthy and I am feel truly blessed to have a second chance to be the mother that they deserve I am proud to say that I am a Christian because He loved me first. All my life I have searched for love and acceptance. What I didn't realize was that it was in front of me the whole time. I am now part of a wonderful Church family and I am finding my way. I am an active member of the Care Ministry. Eventually I will join the choir and begin what I started all those years ago. By the end of my new member's class, I received confirmation about what God wants me to do in this life. I am to tell the people about God and share with them ways to get their lives and houses in order before Jesus returns.

I have also been blessed with true love. It is the real deal this time. We met through a mutual friend and we were completely honest about our past lives. We took our time getting to know each other. This time, I wanted to do everything God's way because I wanted His blessing. We visit one another and my boys have developed a relationship with him.

I had prayed for a God-fearing, equally-yoked man with whom to share my life. I had enough of the wrong kind of man. This time, I wanted him to be a blessing instead of a curse. The Bible states that a man finds a good thing when he finds a wife. I am so glad that he found me. I pray that I will always be just what he wants and need, that I will be his only love, and that he will honor and love me as Christ commanded.

I pray that my story will inspire others to come to the full knowledge and love of Jesus Christ. No matter what you encounter in life, keep pressing on. For your blessing is waiting just on the other side of through. We have all been created with a purpose. It is up to us to stay focused and on the path to our destiny.

God did not promise that our lives would be trouble-free, but He did promise us peace through it all. Rest peacefully, knowing that God has everything under control. When trial arise, Go to the Father first instead of making Him your last resort. He's waiting for us to turn to Him concerning the issues of life, whether good or bad. And remember that there is nothing you can do to separate you from His loving arms. When you accept Him into your life, all condemnation is removed and your transgressions are tossed into the sea of forgetfulness.

Remember to speak positivity into your life and surround yourself with those who love you and want the best for you. Pray for strength and wisdom each day and let God handle the rest. We are all works in progress, so help one another and always love others even when you don't want to. I promise you won't regret it. Be forever blessed.

Thank you for reading my book and I pray that what I have said will give someone hope that any and everything is possible Amen with love and God bless cause I neither take no ownership nor the credit. I owe my life to God and God alone!!!!!!!!!!!!!!!!!

Ms. Maria Antoinette Finney aka Ms. Poochie

My Life Skill's Lesson Q&A

Q. What have I learned through the things that I went through in my early years in life?

a. To always stay focus and that my parents were always right and that they weren't telling me anything wrong. As you grow different things will happen in life but if you always keep God as the head you can do anything. God will give you the desires of your heart. Never allow a person to make choices for you and tell you how your life is supposed to be because they will set standards for you and when you don't meet them, you will be discouraged. When people do that, they are only doing it for themselves and not you.

Q. Why do I feel like family is so important?

a. Family is like a box of sweets and it can also be like a lemon. You all will have good and bad days. Family can have their moments and sometimes it can be like a roller coaster.

It will have its ups and downs, that's what family do. Also family will be there to pick up the pieces when you are broken. Sometimes blood is thicker than water but my motto is a family that prays together will stay together. You should never put anything or anybody in front of family.

Q. How do you come to grips with being raped by a family member or a friend?

a. Pray and you have to forgive. It will hurt and there will be days where it seems as though it was yesterday. Never hold it on the inside because you can hurt yourself and do harm to yourself. Most of all go to God in prayer and ask him to give you the strength to keep pressing forward during your time. If you ever run across that person who raped you, don't allow the enemy to tell you to curse or beat that person. Right where you stand, stretch your arms and look towards heaven and ask God to give you the strength and keep moving. Always forgive and forget and for God's sake, never hold a grudge against them because God will deal with them accordly. Never take matters into your own hands because it will make matters worse then what they already are. Never be afraid to tell someone. Don't just tell someone that you don't trust, tell a family member and go straight to the authority so they can help. Better yet go to a near hospital and they will call the police.

Q. How do you deal with a single parent home?

a. Well you have to first know that it wasn't your fault that your parents aren't together, and it doesn't mean that they love you less cause they still love you with all of their heart. You can call a family meeting and ask the questions and if that doesn't work go to God in prayer. Look at it on the bright side, you will have two homes to go to, and you can still spend time with both of them. You can still have a great relationship with both parents. Always remember that they still love you and sometimes kids can be so ugly to you when they know that your folks aren't together so brush it off anyway. (-.—this statement does not make sense)

Q. How do you deal with when your family is doing things that are illegal?

a. Well if you are young you really don't have much of a say so. Just pray that nothing bad happens to you or your family. But don't worry about what people have to say about you or what your family do. Just walk away and it's not what they call you but it's what you answer to that matters. Yeah you will stand out. If you come into money, you will have friends out of the woods that you didn't even know you had. That's where you can see who is a true friend and who isn't cause they want to be in your life for the wrong reasons (money, clothes, cars and last but not the least, that you would have become very popular).

Q. At what age is a good time to get a boyfriend?

a. Wait until you are 30 lol. Just an inside joke. I can remember said 'that's what my dad said one time about me, but for real I feel like God, education should be what you do and everything else will fall in line later because you don't want to waste your life into doing something that you might and will regret. Keep your head up and stay focus people. But I know if you're going to be dating before 21 you shouldn't be having no sex, foreplay or anything like that until you are married.

Q. What do you do if you get knocked up when you are young?

a. Everything will be alright just don't drop out of school for God's sake. Without an education, you really can't do nothing not even flip burgers. Like my mom told me, the first time you get knocked up, that's a mistake .Then you get knocked up again, you knew what you were doing. Don't have an abortion. That's not a choice or an option. The baby didn't ask to be conceived and it's not fair to them. So the best thing is not to have sex until you are married, thus said The Lord!!!!!

Q. What do you do when the person you are with abuse you?

a. First pray and try to get away from the person. Never stay around and call the Police and have it on record. Don't allow that person to lure you back in. Always let someone know what is going on and never allow them to say they are sorry. Yeah, they are sorry until the next time. Here are some signs to look for: 1.They get mad very easy 2.They start to want to know your every move 3.They start to handle you real rough 4.They start throwing things around when they are mad 5. When they say you are theirs with this pose look on their face 6. When you are in public and you can't even talk to a different sex 7. When they show their true colors when things don't go their way 8. When they want to control everything about you (like they tell you how to handle your business. These are some of the signs. 9. When the opposite sex speak to you and don't speak to them and they get mad. 10. When they are drinking and they can't handle the alcohol, they be thinking that you are talking to someone and they get mad as hell 11. When they look through your cell phone. 12. When they look at your cell phone bill. 13. They also look at the home phone bill to see who you called and who called there. 14. If you all have a Caller ID and they monitor the incoming call. 15. When they be looking at the mileage on your car. Yeah you got some that will do that too to see how far you have driven. 16. When they want to know how long you are going to be gone, where, why and with whom. If you leave them, an ex is an ex for a reason. Never go back and if they don't want to hear the word, "no" then get a court order for them to stay away from you and or your family. We weren't put on this earth to be some man or woman's punching bag!!!!!

Q. Why doing drugs is bad for you?

a. It can kill you. Neither your mind nor your body can function right. Just say no to drugs period. If some tries to make you use drugs, just say nope. Drugs kills your hope, put down the dope. Once you start to use drugs, then 9 out of 10 people can tell because you unfold right before their eyes. You will sell your soul to the Devil and you will lose everything that you have ...you can lose your family, and your own self to drugs. God cannot use you if you are putting toxins in your body. Using drugs you are not in your right mind and you will do just about anything to anybody.

We have all said fox hole prayers saying lawd if you get me out of this I promise I won't pick up and use. If you do go to a NA Meeting, go in there with an open mind and be true to thane's self. You can choose to stay clean. Mine was God and prayers. If anyone reading this, you can do it. Don't give up or give in. God is able to deliver you from anything. Look at me clean for three years. Praise God. Don't give up on God cause he won't give up on you. He's able!!!!

Q. What do you do when all hell seems to break loose?

a. Pray step fast unmovable allows abide in The Word of the Lord and just know that he won't put no more on you that you can bear. You got to be ready for just about anything and always remain open minded at all times and always surround yourself around positive people who gonna keep you up lifted. People who will have your heart at best interest and never tell you anything that will harm you or others. If you do have friends like that, you better hold on tight to those kind of people and never let go!!!

Q. What must you do if you back slide?

a. Go to God in prayer with a clear and open mind. When you go to him, ask forgiveness and he will. He is not man that he shall lie (like woman and man on earth). He is a God of order and we have to make sure that our lives line up with the Word!!!!

Q. What if you go back out into the worldly world?

a. Pray because we're not god, we are only humans and we all will Make Mistakes we have To Pick ourselves up and we Must Try again. Ask god to forgive us once More!!!!!

As I end my Q&A's I want to leave my readers with this. I do this every morning and that is to pray before my feet touch the floor because when you open your eyes and the enemy sees that he be like darn there she goes, I better flee because I can't touch her. Do your normal when you get out the bed and always read your word before your day gets busy, so the Devil won't have no room to come in to attack. You tell the Devil you got the wrong person on the right day because I will bust you in your face and get thee behind me so you need to go back out the way you came in, or else I will kick you out because you are not welcome in this home. I am on the battlefield for my Lord and I promised him that I will serve him till I did. Lord open up the flood gates of heaven let it rain!!! My Prayer for the people of the world is to pray that you have learned something from my book and it has touched you in some form or fashion in your life, and that you will now be able to pick up the broken pieces and allow God in your life and do be blessed and one love!!!!!

Made in the USA
Monee, IL
07 July 2026

56552666R00059